CHARGE YOUR FAITH

A 30-Day Devotional for Your Healing

Joy Aifuwa, PharmD

WESTBOW
PRESS®
A DIVISION OF THOMAS NELSON
& ZONDERVAN

WestBow Press books may be ordered through booksellers or by contacting:

WestBow Press
A Division of Thomas Nelson & Zondervan
1663 Liberty Drive
Bloomington, IN 47403
www.westbowpress.com
1 (866) 928-1240

Scripture taken from the King James Version of the Bible.

Scripture taken from the New King James Version®. Copyright © 1982 by Thomas Nelson. Used by permission. All rights reserved.

Scripture quotations are taken from the Holy Bible, New Living Translation, copyright ©1996, 2004, 2007, 2013, 2015 by Tyndale House Foundation. Used by permission of Tyndale House Publishers, Inc., Carol Stream, Illinois 60188. All rights reserved.

Scripture taken from the Amplified Bible, Copyright © 1954, 1958, 1962, 1964, 1965, 1987 by The Lockman Foundation. Used by permission.

ISBN: 978-1-9736-0436-5 (sc)
ISBN: 978-1-9736-0437-2 (e)

Library of Congress Control Number: 2017914490

Print information available on the last page.

WestBow Press rev. date: 9/29/2017

DAY 1   SERVING THE LORD

> So you shall serve the LORD your God, and He will bless your bread and your water. And I will take sickness away from the midst of you. (Exodus 23:25 NKJV)

Did you know that God loves you more than anything and desires to heal every sickness or disease you've been diagnosed with? Yes, it's true. God declares in the above verse that if you will serve Him, He will bless your bread (any type of food you eat) and water (including beverages other than water). What does it mean to serve Him? It is more than going to church every Sunday or reading your Bible daily. Serving the Lord involves you having a living relationship with His Son Jesus Christ and making yourself available to Him to be used by Him to affect your friends, family, neighborhood, nation, and even the rest of the world. As you develop in your relationship with Jesus and read your Bible daily, the life of God will begin to flow into you to direct your steps, and the healing power of God will cause healing to take place in your body. If you are ready to serve the Lord, please repeat the following prayer out loud:

> Dear heavenly Father, today I receive Your Son, Jesus Christ, as my Lord and Savior. I believe that He died for me on the cross and that He cleansed me of all my sins. I believe that Jesus is my healer. I present myself to You this day and make the commitment to serve You and obey Your Word. Teach me how to live for You. I pray this now in Jesus's name. Amen.

Scripture reading: Exodus 23:20–26; Romans 12:1–2

DAY 2   PEACE OF MIND

You will keep him in perfect peace, whose mind is stayed on You, because he trusts in You. (Isaiah 26:3 NKJV)

Do you often lie in bed, unable to sleep because of racing or worried thoughts about a particular problem you're facing? God has the solution you need. When you choose to focus on Him instead of the problem you're facing, He promises to give you peace of mind and of heart. Well, you may say, "That's so easy to say but difficult to do!" It does take some effort, but God will help you if you're determined. Every time that worried thought comes up, read the above scripture out loud and thank the Lord for the blessings you currently have. Praise Him for giving you another day to live and for sending His Son, Jesus. Thank Him for your family, job, home, and so forth. Tell Him something you're grateful for, and meditate on Him. Praise will command the attention of God, who will, in return, calm the restlessness in your mind and heart and move on your behalf to deliver you from the problems you're facing. If you're ready for peace of mind, pray the following prayer out loud:

> Dear heavenly Father, Your Word tells me that if I fix my mind on You and put my trust in You, You will give me perfect peace. I commit to You now this problem I'm facing—[fill in the blank]. I thank You for giving me Your perfect peace and moving on my behalf to deliver me. I receive Your perfect peace now in Jesus's name. Amen.

Scripture reading: Leviticus 26:6; Isaiah 26:3–4; Psalm 149:1–9; 1 Peter 5:6–7

DAY 3   PRAISE: THE KEY TO OPENING PRISON DOORS

> But at midnight Paul and Silas were praying and singing hymns to God, and the prisoners were listening to them. Suddenly there was a great earthquake, so that the foundations of the prison were shaken; and immediately all the doors were open and everyone's chains were loosed. (Acts 16:25–26 NKJV)

Paul and Silas were living testimonies of God's faithfulness to send help when His people simply praise Him. They had been beaten severely and thrown into a dirty, dingy prison, with their feet fastened in stocks, because they preached about Jesus Christ. As their lives flashed before them, they could have cried their hearts out, asking why this was happening to them. Instead, they prayed and sang hymns to God, and they did it so everyone around them could hear! And God came down swiftly and caused there to be an earthquake so fierce that all the prison doors flew open and their chains came loose. Now that's power!

Although Paul and Silas were in a physical prison, there are many people who experience perpetual prison in other ways. Some experience it emotionally, constantly battling thoughts of depression, suicide, or anxiety. Others are in prison in the relationships in which they are trapped. Others experience the prison of always been sick and never getting better. If you can relate to any one of these, praising God is the key to your prison doors being opened and the chains on your mind being loosed. Open your mouth and begin to thank the Lord for giving you the air that you breathe, for preserving your life during that car accident, for waking you up in your right mind, and for giving you another day to start over. Praise Him for how great He is, and put your confidence in His ability to rescue you from your prison. And as you continue to praise Him, you won't remain down or sick for long. Meditating on the book of Psalms will give you great insight on the power of praise. Please pray the following prayer out loud:

> Dear heavenly Father, I come to You in the name of Jesus, asking You for the grace to praise You more. Your Word demonstrates the power of praise to get me out of the prison I am in. I refuse to tolerate any more thoughts of depression, anxiety, fear, sickness, and so forth. I now receive Your grace to praise You and thank You for delivering me from my situation. I declare that I am free from now on, in Jesus's name.

Scripture reading: Psalm 68:1–8, 77:1–20; Isaiah 61:1–3; Acts 16:25–26

DAY 4   JESUS THE HEALER

How God anointed Jesus of Nazareth with the Holy Ghost and with power: who went about doing good and healing all that were oppressed of the devil; for God was with Him. (Acts 10:38 KJV)

If you ask most people who Jesus Christ was, they may tell you that He was a great leader or prophet whose teachings people still follow today. Others may say they believe Jesus to have died on the cross and risen again and that believing in Him will cause them to escape hell and go to heaven. This is all true, but there's much more to Him than that. Jesus, God the Son, was anointed of God the Father with the Holy Ghost or Holy Spirit to heal people who were oppressed of the devil. People were oppressed of the devil in many forms: by physical illness or deformities, by demonic influences causing some to act abnormal, by fear, or by death. Jesus's mission while He was on the earth was to minister to people that He was anointed with the power of the Holy Spirit to heal them; and those who believed His words were healed, delivered, and set free.

The Bible says in Hebrews 13:8 (NKJV) that "Jesus Christ is the same yesterday, and today and forever." You see, Jesus is still alive today, and it is still His will to heal you. You may be oppressed by the devil in the form of family trouble, a terminal illness, a rebellious child, or any other thing that's draining you spiritually, emotionally, physically, or financially. Maybe you're even buried in debt, and you're feeling stressed out. I'm here to tell you that there is hope. Jesus Christ loves you. He died for you on the cross and rose again so that He could obliterate whatever is choking you in any area of your life and restore you back to health, peace, love, and joy. When He lay there on that cross, every sickness that humankind would ever be afflicted with was placed on Him so that you wouldn't have to carry it. When He arose, He made healing available for all who needed it. Right after He ascended to heaven, the book of Acts recorded numerous accounts of God's healing power in action as Jesus's disciples went about preaching in the name of Jesus. Here's how you access Jesus the healer—by accepting Jesus Christ as your Lord and Savior. Please repeat the following prayer out loud:

> Dear heavenly Father, I believe You sent Your Son, Jesus Christ, to die on the cross for me and that He bore all my sicknesses, diseases, and the troubles I'm facing. I believe that He rose again and has made His Holy Spirit available to me. I receive Jesus as my Lord and Savior as well as my healer. I receive Your healing power now regarding this issue: [fill in the blank]. And I now thank You for my healing. I pray this prayer in Jesus's name. Amen.

Scripture reading: Luke 4:17–21; Acts 10:38; Hebrews 2:9–15

DAY 5   THE NAME OF JESUS

> Therefore God also has highly exalted Him and given Him the name which is above every name, that at the name of Jesus every knee should bow, of those in heaven, and of those on earth, and of those under the earth, and that every tongue should confess that Jesus Christ is Lord, to the glory of God the Father. (Philippians 2:9–11 NKJV)

The name of Jesus is one of the most powerful weapons to use in receiving your healing. The Bible says that the name Jesus Christ is above every other name in heaven, earth, and hell. Things on earth that have names are people, places, things, and medical conditions or medical terminology about that condition. This means that depression, anxiety, arthritis, high blood sugar, cancer, and so forth have to obey and leave your mind or body the moment the name Jesus Christ is declared over that disease. Sometimes you may experience immediate results in your body and begin to feel better right away, while other times it may look like nothing is happening. Many people with diseases of long continuance may even be discouraged and think that it's too good to be true for them to ever feel better.

If you fall into this category, don't allow fear to rob you of your healing. Jesus died not only to rescue you from the power of sin and spiritual death, but He also made healing available for you: in your spirit, your soul (your mind, will, and emotions), and your body. The moment you speak the name of Jesus over your situation, that's the moment His healing power begins to work, even though you may not feel anything right away. Whatever ails you today, whether it's a slight headache, anxiety, depression, or a terminal illness, believe in the name of Jesus and speak His name over your body and mind. Please repeat the following prayer out loud:

> Dear heavenly Father, I come to You, in the name of Jesus Christ, to receive my healing. Your Word tells me that the name of Jesus is above every name in heaven, earth, and hell, so therefore, it is above my situation (fill in the blank). I declare the name of Jesus over this situation I'm experiencing (fill in the blank), and I declare that I am healed now, in Jesus's name. I now thank You for my healing and will continue to praise You daily for it. Amen.

After you've prayed this prayer, spend time praising Him daily, thanking Him for the healing you've received by faith. Stick with it. God's Word never fails.

Scripture reading: Psalms 103:1–5; Luke 10:1–17; Philippians 2:1–11

DAY 6 THE HOLY SPIRIT: GOD'S POWER AGENT FOR CREATIVE MIRACLES

> And the angel answered and said unto her, The Holy Spirit shall come upon you, and the power of the Highest will overshadow you; therefore also that Holy One who is to be born will be called the Son of God. (Luke 1:35 NKJV)

The Holy Spirit, God's power agent, is the third person of the Godhead or Holy Trinity (God the Father, God the Son [Jesus Christ], and God the Holy Spirit). Just as man is a three-part being made up of spirit, soul, and body (1 Thessalonians 5:23), God is likewise. In Genesis 1:1, before men and women existed, the Bible tells us that after God created heaven and earth and the earth became an empty waste, the Spirit of God moved upon the face of the waters. Genesis 1:3 (NKJV) states, "And God said, let there be light: and there was light." John 1:1–2 (NKJV) states, "In the beginning was the Word [referring to Jesus] and the Word was with God and the Word was God. The same was in the beginning with God." When God spoke the words that released His light energy on the earth, the Father, the Son, and the Holy Spirit were present.

A similar creative miracle occurred in Mary in Luke 1:38 (NKJV), when the angel Gabriel told her that she would give birth to the Son of God although she was a virgin. When she agreed with the words that the angel spoke by saying, "Let it be to me according to your word," it enabled the Holy Spirit to perform the creative miracle of sending Jesus, who was then in heaven with the Father, to come in the form of a baby to be birthed by a virgin.

The Holy Spirit is still available to you today and is working creative miracles in anyone who will believe the Word of God concerning their healing. You receive the Holy Spirit the moment you say, "Jesus is Lord. I accept Jesus as my Lord and Savior." If you're dealing with missing limbs, amputations, or a disfiguring disease, the power of God is available to you to restore you and make you completely whole. Please pray the following prayer out loud:

> Heavenly Father, I come to You in the name of Jesus. I thank You for making the Holy Spirit available to me. I receive my creative miracle over my condition (fill in the blank) based on Your Word and thank You for my restoration in Jesus's name. Amen.

Spend time meditating on the Word daily, and God will confirm His Word with miracles.
Scripture reading: Genesis 1:1–3; Matthew 12:9–13; Luke 1:26–38

DAY 7   LEARNING TO LAUGH MORE

A merry heart does good, like medicine, but a broken spirit dries the bones.
(Proverbs 17:22 NKJV)

It's a well-known concept that laughter makes you feel better, but God's Word goes further to explain that it is good for you because it acts like medicine. Scientifically speaking, there have been studies that show that laughing, especially a deep belly laugh, releases chemicals in the body, known as endorphins, that make you feel better and raise your pain threshold, enabling your body to feel less pain. Many people deal with a broken spirit (also known as a broken heart) as a result of failed relationships or hurt from a relationship, death in the family, and more. A person dealing with a broken heart ends up sick because it affects the body in detrimental ways. Since brokenness is connected with a feeling of stress, increased amounts of stress hormone, called cortisol, are released. This raises blood pressure and blood sugar as well as impairs the ability to form bones. People dealing with emotional hurt often also suffer from anxiety, which raises the heart rate and eventually blood pressure. So you see, God is wise in instructing you and me to have a merry heart.

You may say, "I hear what you're saying, but you don't know what I'm facing or what I've been through." It's true that no two situations are alike. There may be times when you're so hurt that you see no way out. I've been there as well. Instead of spending time dwelling on what you're going through, engage in activities that make you laugh. If it's a favorite show that makes you laugh, watch it. If taking a long walk across nature brings enjoyment and entertains you, do more of it. Learn to laugh more. Find something that brings you joy. Please pray the following prayer out loud:

> Dear heavenly Father, I come to You in the name of Jesus because I need healing from a broken heart due to this broken situation (fill in the blank). I receive Jesus as the healer of my broken heart and thank You for helping me laugh more so I may be healed. I forgive whoever hurt me and put this hurtful situation behind me now in Jesus's name. Amen.

Scripture reading: Genesis 21:5–7; Proverbs 17:22; Ecclesiastes 3:1–4; Isaiah 12:1–6

DAY 8   HOW GOD DEALS WITH SHAME OR DEEP HURT

> Looking unto Jesus, the author and finisher of our faith, who for the joy that was set before Him endured the cross, despising the shame, and has sat down at the right hand of the throne of God. For consider Him who endured such hostility from sinners against Himself, lest you become weary and discouraged in your souls. (Hebrew 12:2–3 NKJV)

To the general population, God is impersonal. They picture Him at a great distance high up in the sky and often have difficulty relating to Him, particularly where their emotions are concerned. The Bible says in Genesis 1:27 (NKJV), "So God created man in His own image, in the image of God created He him; male and female created He them." We were created with His divine DNA, and the reason that you and I have emotions is because He too has emotions. Isn't that amazing? This may come as a surprise to you, but God the Father and God the Son, Jesus, know what it's like to experience shame and deep emotional hurt. Jesus has also experienced being rejected, being made fun of, and despised. In the above scripture, When Jesus hung there on the cross for all mankind, He was mocked, spit at, punched in the face, and bruised physically and emotionally. Jesus endured all the shame, sin, sickness, and disease you and I would ever face because of this phrase from the above passage: "Who for the joy that was set before Him …"

In fact, I was going through a difficult emotional period and I asked the Lord one day, "Lord, how do You deal with a broken heart? I know You are hurt when Your children reject You."

And do you know what He said? He said, "Find something that brings you joy," and brought the above passage of scripture to my remembrance. Jesus endured such inhumane suffering at the cross because He had His eyes set on something that brought Him joy: fulfilling His Father's eternal purpose to give eternal life to as many as would believe in Him.

Draw closer to the Lord. Picture Jesus sitting next to you and tell Him your shame, hurt, or pain. Picture Jesus on that cross where He bore in His body all that you're going through. Please pray this prayer out loud:

> Dear heavenly Father, I come to You in Jesus's name and give you the burden of (fill in the blank) I've been carrying. I believe that Jesus bore it on the cross, and this situation is no longer mine to struggle with. Teach me how to focus on what brings me joy instead of what hurts me. Thank You for my healing and joy. I receive them now in Jesus's name. Amen.

Scripture reading: Isaiah 53: 1–5; John 17:1–24; Hebrews 12:1–3; I Peter 5:6–7

DAY 9   THE TENDER SIDE OF GOD

> O Jerusalem, Jerusalem, the one who kills the prophets and stones those who are sent to her! How often I wanted to gather your children together, as a hen gathers her chicks under her wings, but you were not willing! (Matthew 23:37 NKJV)

Have you every observed a mom and dad with their baby or young child? You've probably noticed that they play with their child by tickling, swaying back and forth, or entertaining their little one. Imagine the depth of love a parent has for his or her child and how much that parent wants to express his or her deep love. Well, God is like that at a much greater level than any earthly parent. His love is so deep, vast, unwavering, and faithful.

Many people are suffering today from anxiety, PTSD, depression, or other health problems because of their childhood experiences. Some have never let go of the painful memories of how their parents or legal guardian mistreated, ignored, molested, or rejected them.

God wants to be a parent to you—not one who criticizes you or demeans you but one who will love you, protect you, and tenderly care for you. He wants to hide you in His secret place of protection so that no spiritual, emotional, or physical harm can come near you. He yearns to be close to you and me, to share things with us that we need to know about Him and ourselves, as well as give us direction for our lives. He enjoys it when we commune with Him as we sing to Him, talk and listen to Him, pray to Him, and read His Word.

God is the perfect parent you've been missing and longing for your whole life. He wants to not only make you feel better when you're bruised but He wants to heal those deep roots of hurt, bitterness, fear, and distrust that stemmed from your childhood or happened later in life. Allow Him to show you His tender side. Please pray the following prayer out loud:

> Dear heavenly Father, I come to You in the name of Jesus and give you the care of the painful memories of my past that have caused me to feel rejected and hurt. I receive my healing and believe that You love me and want to adopt me as Your child. I give You my life, and I believe You are a good Father and will love and care for me. Thank You for being a good example of what a parent should be and teaching me how to be a good parent to my children in Jesus's name. Amen.

Scripture reading: Matthew 23:37–38; Luke 13:34; Romans 8:14–17

DAY 10   YOUR WORDS CAN MAKE YOU OR BREAK YOU

A wholesome tongue is a tree of life, but perverseness in it breaks the spirit.
(Proverbs 15:4 NKJV)

The spirit of a man will sustain him in sickness, but who can bear a broken spirit?
(Proverbs 18:14 NKJV)

Have you ever been affected by negative, hurtful words someone said to you in the past? We all have. Words can have a positive or negative impact in our lives, especially when those words come from someone we highly respect or look up to. Many people are still replaying in their mind words their mentor or parent may have said to them over a decade ago. Words can determine your progress or failure in life, particularly words you repeat about yourself over and over again. The Bible says that a wholesome tongue (a tongue filled with kind words that uplift people) is a tree of life. When you speak kind words to a person, they have a healing effect in that individual's spirit, soul, and body. You may have experienced this at least once before when you were having a bad day, and someone came to you and gave you a word of encouragement, and it lifted your mood. You may also have noticed that the particular level of stress you were under at that moment went away.

You may be familiar with the importance of speaking kindly to and about other people, but there is another key point often missed. Most people scarcely pay attention to the words that they speak over themselves. They look in the mirror every day and say things such as, "My hair looks so ugly today," or, "I look so fat," or, "I'm such a failure." These negative words are not uplifting; instead, they break the spirit. By saying such things, you reject yourself without even knowing it and set yourself up for failure. Each time you repeat those negative words, you begin to believe them, and they will eventually affect how you think. Depression, anxiety, panic attacks, difficulty losing weight, and a failure mindset are often the result of speaking negatively about yourself.

The next time you start speaking negative words over yourself or over the problems you're currently facing, immediately correct yourself and say this: "Lord, I thank You for loving me just as I am. Thank You that You find no flaw in me. I am perfect in your sight. Body, you are beautiful, fearfully and wonderfully made, and I dedicate you to the Lord." Say it over and over again until you begin to believe it. Speak life words, not death words, over yourself.

Scripture reading: Proverbs 15:1–4; Proverbs 18:14–21; Matthew 12:33–37

DAY 11   FORGIVENESS: A MISSING INGREDIENT TO YOUR HEALING

> Let all bitterness, wrath, anger, clamor, and evil speaking be put away from you, with all malice. And be kind to one another, tenderhearted, forgiving one another, even as God in Christ forgave you. (Ephesians 4:31–32 NKJV)

Have you ever had an argument with someone that resulted in the exchange of bitter, hateful words, words you regret were ever spoken by you or the other person? The Bible warns us not speak harshly to one another but instead to be kind and forgive. Think about the cascade of events that occur when you speak to someone out of spite or rage: first, a broken fellowship now exists between you and the other individual. Next, you become anxious, and your heart races every time you think about that person and what he or she said to you. As you continue to rehearse the argument in your mind, you grow bitter toward that individual and even begin telling other people about it. Meanwhile, you've probably begun to notice that your blood pressure is higher than it normally is or you may experience a higher level of anxiety than you did before.

God commands us to be kind to one another and walk in a state of forgiveness because He knows how it affects our physical bodies. According to a quote by Dr. Karen Swartz from Johns Hopkins University, "Chronic anger puts you into a fight-or-flight mode which results in numerous changes in heart rate, blood pressure, immune response. Those changes, then, increase the risk of depression, heart disease, diabetes, among other conditions. Forgiveness, however, calms stress levels, leading to improved health." [1]

So if you're at odds with someone today, don't wait another minute. Call, text, e-mail, or Skype that individual, and do your best to reconcile with him or her. Even if you were not at fault, do it. Your health is impacted by it. Please pray this:

> Dear heavenly Father, I come to You in Jesus's name to confess my sin of unforgiveness and receive my forgiveness. By faith, I forgive (fill in the blank) for what he or she said or did to me, and I now let go of any offense I have toward this person. Please teach me how to forgive others the way You forgave me of all my sins. I also receive healing in my mind and body now and thank You for it in Jesus's name. Amen.

Scripture reading: Mark 11:22–27; Ephesians 4:26–32

---

[1] "Healthy Aging." *Forgiveness: Your Health Depends on It.* Johns Hopkins University. Web. 5 June 2017. www.hopkinsmedicine.org/health/healthy_agin/healthy_connections/forgiveness-your-health-depends-on-it

DAY 12 THE LIFE-GIVING SPIRIT OF GOD

> But if the Spirit of Him who raised Jesus from the dead dwells in you, He who raised Christ from the dead will also give life to your mortal bodies through His Spirit who dwells in you. (Romans 8:11 NKJV)

The Bible states that when Jesus died on the cross, the Spirit of God or the Holy Spirit raised Him up from the dead. Likewise, when you believe that Jesus was raised from the dead, that same Spirit of God will live inside of you, and He will also give life to your physical body. Jesus said in John 6:63 (NKJV) that "it is the Spirit who gives life; the flesh profits nothing. The words that I speak to you are spirit and they are life." The life of God is where the healing that you need can be found, and His Word is the source of that life for you and me. The Bible is not merely comprised of writers who were led of the Holy Spirit to write; every word actually contains the DNA of God. In other words, every word in the Bible is saturated with the life-giving power of God to heal you.

If you're suffering from arthritis, joint or muscle stiffness, or any other sickness or disease, there is great hope for you. God wants you healed from the top of your head to the soles of your feet. He wants every stubborn disease that has left you crippled to leave your body and desires to make you completely whole. His will is not for you to be suffering from the side effects of your medications, especially the ones that greatly affect your quality of life. His Holy Spirit was made available to you over two thousand years ago, when Jesus Christ was raised from the dead; and when you receive Jesus as your Lord and Savior, the power of God is made available to you. Ask Jesus to come into your heart today if you haven't already done so. Tap into the life-giving Spirit of God. Please pray the following prayer out loud:

> Dear heavenly Father, today I receive Jesus as my Lord and Savior. I believe that He was raised from the dead by the Spirit of God, and today I receive You, precious Holy Spirit. I receive the life of God, which makes me whole: spirit, soul, and body. I thank You for my healing in this area of my life (fill in the blank). I receive it now in Jesus's name. Amen.

Scripture reading: John 6:63; Romans 8:1–11; 2 Timothy 3:14–17

DAY 13   WHAT REALLY TOOK PLACE AT THE CROSS

> Therefore I also, after I heard of your faith in the Lord Jesus and love for all the saints, do not cease to give thanks for you, making mention of you in my prayers: that the God of our Lord Jesus Christ, the Father of glory may give to you the spirit of wisdom and revelation in the knowledge of Him ... and what is the exceeding greatness of His power toward us who believe, according to the working of His mighty power which He worked in Christ when He raised Him from dead and seated Him at His right hand in the heavenly places. (Ephesians 1:15–19 NKJV)

Do you remember those cartoons you watched when you were a child, where a cartoon character would light dynamite and there was a tremendously loud explosion? People with scientific backgrounds have a level of comprehension of the magnitude of energy that is released in such an explosion. In the above scripture, the apostle Paul is praying that the believers at the church of Ephesus would comprehend "what is the exceeding greatness of His power toward us who believe, according to the working of His mighty power which He worked in Christ when He raised Him from the dead and seated Him." He prayed that you and I would develop a deep understanding of the dynamic, explosive, miracle-working power of God, which raised Jesus from the dead, and which caused you to be born again when you received Jesus as your Lord and Savior.

The "exceeding greatness of His power" can also be called "wonder-working power," because of the magnitude of force it exerts and releases. It is powerful enough to obliterate even the most challenging, life-threatening diseases. Many people classify ailments in degrees; a headache is barely alarming because it can be easily treated, but cancer raises great fear because it is a very aggressive disease. God's power is much more aggressive than any illness you're facing. In fact, in these days, God wants to demonstrate His mighty resurrection power to you and me. Nothing is too hard for God to take care of. Put your trust in Him. Allow Him to reveal the strength of His right arm. Please pray the following prayer out loud:

> Dear heavenly Father, I come to You in the name of Jesus to receive a deeper understanding of the mighty power of God that's available to me to heal my spirit, soul, and body. You are a big God, and I believe that my condition (fill in the blank) is not too hard for You to take care of. I receive my healing now, and I thank You for demonstrating Your mighty power in my life in Jesus's name. Amen.

Scripture reading: Romans 6:1–4; Ephesians 1:15–21; Ephesians 1:1–7

DAY 14 | THE GLORY OF GOD

> Then your light shall break forth like the morning, your healing shall spring forth speedily, and your righteousness shall go before you; the glory of the Lord shall be your rear guard. (Isaiah 58:8 NKJV)

The glory of God is the presence of God manifested in a physical form, which can be seen or felt. It is also His power and goodness revealed to mankind. When God led the children of Israel through the wilderness, the Lord "went before them by day in a pillar of cloud to lead the way, and by night in a pillar of fire to give them light" (Exodus 13:20–21 NKJV). In 2 Chronicles 5:13–14 (NKJV), when Solomon dedicated the temple to the Lord, "the priests could not continue ministering because of the cloud: for the glory of the Lord had filled the house of God." Also, when Moses asked God to reveal His glory to him in Exodus 33:18, the Lord revealed that His glory was His attributes: "merciful and gracious, long-suffering, abundant in goodness and truth" (Exodus 34:6 NKJV). Simply put, the glory of God reveals what God is heavy with; He is heavy with power, goodness, healing, wealth, signs and wonders, and more.

You may ask, what is the purpose of His glory? It is to reveal Himself to you so that you may know that He is real. One major aspect of His glory that you and I can be affected by is His healing power. In fact, when His presence is near, healing will take place. You may or may not notice it right away, but when His glory manifests, there will be a change in your physical condition.

How can the glory of God be made available to you? When you praise and worship Him. The Bible says in Psalm 22:3 (KJV) that He inhabits the praises of His people. Begin to praise Him today, right where you are. Praise Him for His goodness and His great love for you. Praise Him when you feel like it and when you don't feel like it. Make it a practice to spend time with Him daily in praise and worship. As you do that, His manifest presence will heal your body.

Scripture reading: 2 Chronicles 5:1–14; 2 Chronicles 7:1–3; Psalm 22:1–3; Isaiah 35:1–6; Isaiah 58:1–8

DAY 15   REGAINING YOUR LOST MEMORY

The memory of the righteous is blessed, but the name of the wicked will rot.
(Proverbs 10:7 NKJV)

For "who has known the mind of the LORD that he may instruct Him?" But we
have the mind of Christ. (1 Corinthians 2:15–16 NKJV)

One of the biggest problems people are facing today, particularly the elderly, is difficulty remembering things. The rate of newly diagnosed cases of dementia and other memory impairments has grown rapidly and is prevalent among the elderly today. They go from being active in their community to being barely able to take care of themselves. If you're facing such a situation or know someone who is, there is good news for you. The Bible says that the "memory of the righteous is blessed." If you're walking with God and living upright, not only will your name have a good reputation among people, but God will see to it that you age gracefully and retain your memory even in old age. Just in case you're not convinced, the second passage of scripture above explains that if you're a Christian and have the Holy Spirit living inside of your heart, you have access to the mind of the Lord or the mind of Christ. Through Jesus, you have access to knowing the things of God, which He wants to reveal to you in order to prosper you and give you good health. In the same manner, you have the ability to think the way God thinks, to know what He has planned for your life and the amazing things He wants to use you to accomplish for His glory.

How many of you know that God does not have a memory problem? He knows everything about everything and never misses a beat. He knows how to cook, clean, drive a car, style hair, and clothe you. He knows where those missing keys are that you misplaced. He still remembers what you said to Him when you were a little child. If you ask Him, He can tell you the name of your first kindergarten teacher. He was there that day when you cried over that person who hurt you, and He knows the events that happened in your life at a young age that have greatly affected you today. What am I trying to say? That you have access to a God who can help you through any memory problems you're facing and help you regain your lost memories.

So today, stop saying, "I have dementia," or "I can't remember." Instead, say, "Lord, I can't recall this particular thing right now, but I thank You that my memory is blessed. I have the mind of Christ, and I receive supernatural recall of my lost memories now in Jesus's name. Amen." Remind yourself of this every day.

Scripture reading: John 16:12–15; 1 Corinthians 2:6–16; 1 John 2:18–20

DAY 16   PRAYING FOR YOUR ENEMIES

> But I say to you who hear: Love your enemies, do good to those who hate you, bless those who curse you, and pray for those who spitefully use you. (Luke 6:27–28 NKJV)

Every person on this planet has been mistreated by someone in one way or the other. You may have been betrayed by someone you trusted or someone you knew may have threatened you or your family. Others may have gossiped about you and spread deleterious rumors about you to malign your character. Some people can't even stand to be in the same room as their family members because of family grudges. Jesus tells us in the above scripture that we are to love our enemies and pray for them. Doesn't that sound completely foolish? I mean, what sense does it make to love people who do you harm and try to ruin your life? Because whether or not your body will be in a state of health is determined by how you react to and treat your enemies.

You see, you and I don't have any control over the people who are rude to us and try do us harm, but we do have complete control over how we react to their actions. When you choose to love your enemies, do good to them, bless them, and pray for them, you create an environment for healing to take place in your own body. You don't become stressed out and anxious over that person; instead, you're peaceful and calm. Forgiveness toward that person can then manifest, and you're no longer concerning yourself with what he or she did to you. Also, when you have this attitude toward your enemy, you give God the opportunity to deal with that person, to help him or her become transformed into a better individual.

Practically speaking, how do we do what Jesus has commanded us to do? Train yourself to always speak kindly about your enemies, no matter what they have done to you. If you see that they are in need, do what you can to help them. Every time that negative thought about what they did to you comes to mind, pray for them. Often, people hurt others because they are hurt themselves. Be sensitive to them and try to see from their perspective, if possible. Just a touch of love from you can make a significant difference in their lives. It also helps you remain in a state of peace, free from anxiety and other complications in the body resulting from strife, stress, and unforgiveness. Please pray this out loud:

> Dear heavenly Father, I come to You in the name of Jesus to cast the care of my burdens to You. From this day forward, I make the quality decision to forgive (fill in the blank) for what they did to me or my family. I choose from now on to love them, do good to them, and pray for them. I pray for their healing, and I receive healing in my own body as well. I release them from this offense now in Jesus's name. Amen.

Scripture reading: Matthew 5:43–48; Luke 6:27–36; Romans 12:14

DAY 17 UNFORGIVENESS: A MAJOR HINDRANCE TO YOUR HEALING

And forgive us our sins, as we have forgiven those who sin against us. (Matthew 6:12 New Living Translation)

So He asked them, "why do you question this in your hearts? Is it easier to say 'Your sins are forgiven', or 'Stand up and walk?' So I will prove to you that the Son of Man has the authority on earth to forgive sins. Then Jesus turned to the paralyzed man and said, 'Stand up, pick up your mat, and go home!" (Luke 5:22–24 NLT)

By now, you've heard a lot about the importance of forgiveness and how it affects the body in a positive way. Another aspect of it is revealed in the above passages. In the first passage, Jesus taught His disciples to have an attitude of forgiveness so that they could receive God's forgiveness as well. The two go hand in hand. Then the second passage illustrates how, when Jesus (as God's representative) forgave the paralyzed man his sins, he was immediately healed and could walk.

Picture a large fish tank or aquarium full of water, and imagine all kinds of different fish swimming along the current generated by the power source. Imagine big fish, little fish, colorful fish, or not-so-colorful ones. Likewise, the tank of God's blessings for you contains forgiveness, healing, prosperity, love, joy, and more. It's the same current (God's power) that flows throughout the entire tank so that His forgiveness is available to you the same way healing is available to you. When you forgive others, you give God the ability to be able to forgive you. And the power of God that's released for your forgiveness is the same power for your healing.

Now that you're beginning to understand how vital forgiveness is, find purpose in your heart to be quick to forgive. Forgive your friends, boss, spouse, children, and your local and national politicians. Don't hold offense against anyone. Every time you feel an offense stirring up in you, immediately say, "Lord, I forgive them. I pray that You heal them in the areas where they are challenged, and I bless them in Jesus's name." Keep practicing an attitude of forgiveness daily and thereby receive your own healing daily.

Scripture reading: Matthew 6:9–15; Luke 5:17–25; James 1:19–21

DAY 18   ANSWERS TO YOUR FAILURES

The Spirit of the LORD is upon Me, because He has anointed Me to preach the gospel to the poor; He has sent Me to heal the brokenhearted, to proclaim liberty to the captives and recovery of sight to the blind, to set at liberty those who are oppressed, to proclaim the acceptable year of the Lord. (Luke 4:18–19 NKJV)

But thanks be to God, who gives us the victory through our Lord Jesus Christ. (1 Corinthians 15:57 NKJV)

Most of us display our victories, without reservation, for others to see. We hang plaques of certificates achieved on our walls and place trophies in visible places for viewers to observe and admire. Failures, however, are filed away, in hopes that others never discover them. If you're secretly broken from failures in your past or you are currently dealing with a failed relationship, marriage, business, or any other type of failure, Jesus is here to heal you. He is the healer of the brokenhearted, which encompasses everything that causes your heart to be broken.

Jesus invites everyone brokenhearted from failure, and those who are distressed, worried, and anxious about their futures, to "come to Me, all you who labor and are heavy laden, and I will give you rest. Take My Yoke upon you and learn from Me, for I am gentle and lowly in heart, and you will find rest for your souls. For My yoke is easy and My burden is light" (Matthew 11:28–20 NKJV). When you come to Him, tell Him the areas of failure that you're confronted with. Be open with Him. He wants you to share every problem with Him, not because He doesn't already know them, but because He wants to help you overcome them. He wants to give a different strategy you haven't tried before or a different course of action to take to succeed this time around. He wants to be involved in the littlest thing in your life as well as in the biggest thing in your life.

Jesus has all the answers you need to turn your situation around and achieve victory. First Corinthians 15:57 (NKJV) tells us that God gives us victory through Jesus Christ. You can succeed the first time you do something, without having to experience multiple failed attempts. Even when you don't initially achieve your desired goal, the Lord will give you more and more insight into the situation to get a different outcome the next time around. Jesus is available to heal the pain of failure and to provide you the answers that you need to be victorious. Please pray this prayer out loud:

Dear heavenly Father, I present to You every failure and struggle I have dealt with or am dealing with, and I lay them down before You. I now receive Your healing, Your rest, Your peace, Your joy, and Your insight. Please fill my mind with the wisdom that I need to be victorious in this situation. I receive the answers now in Jesus's name.

The next thing to do now is take a pencil and paper, sit quietly before the Lord, and hear from Him. Trust Him to be faithful to you. He will not disappoint you.

Scripture reading: Matthew 11:28–30; Luke 4:18–19; 1 Corinthians 15:57; 2 Corinthians 2:14

DAY 19 THE STRENGTH OF JOY

My brethren, count it all joy when you fall into various trials. (James 1:2 NKJV)

Do not sorrow, for the joy of the Lord is your strength. (Nehemiah 8:10 NKJV)

Have you ever faced a difficult situation that weighed so heavily upon you that you literally felt drained of energy? You replayed the situation in your head over and over again, searching for a solution, but instead, all you ended up with was a racing heartbeat and a terrible headache. When you're in the midst of a circumstance from which you see no escape, the Bible instructs you to "count it all joy."

You may ask, "What is joy?" Joy is much more than being happy. It is part of fruit of the Holy Spirit, which is deposited into the heart of every Christian. Joy goes beyond what mere happiness can do. Happiness is present in the heart when something favorable occurs or when people are in a good mood, but joy can be present even in difficult circumstances. Because joy emerges from the Spirit of God, it will literally strengthen you by giving you hope that God can and will work things out for you.

Here's an illustration of what I am talking about: You get a phone call that something terrible has happened to your loved one and he or she has been rushed to the hospital. All of a sudden, you're thrown into an unexpected circumstance, and fear, worry, and anxiousness have now accompanied you. Any happiness you had enjoyed the day before is now gone, and you may even begin to despair. What can you do in such a situation to strengthen your heart and prepare yourself for what you're about to face? This is the time to stir up the joy of the Lord inside of you. Before you do anything else, take a few minutes to focus your attention on the Lord. Tell Him how much you love Him, how faithful He is, and that You know He will preserve your loved one's life. Thank Him for all the times He came through for you in the past, and thank Him for what you're expecting Him to do for your loved one. As you do this repeatedly, God will fill your heart with hope that things will work out, and this hope will be your source of joy. Every time you think about the situation, tell yourself, "My God will take care of it!" Watch the worry, fear, and anxiety disappear. Joy is something you have to stir up yourself and is not based on outward circumstances. Stir it up daily, and it will renew your strength daily. Please pray the following prayer out loud:

Dear heavenly Father, I come to You in the name of Jesus and lay down this distressing situation before you. I thank You that Your joy has been deposited into my heart by the Holy Spirit who lives in me. I stir it up now as I thank You for delivering me or this person (fill in the blank) out of this situation. I have hope that nothing is too difficult for You to handle, and I receive the strength that Your joy provides me now in Jesus's name. Amen.

Scripture reading: Nehemiah 8:9–10; Galatians 5:22; Philippians 1:1–25; James 1:1–6

DAY 20   ELIMINATING GRIEF

> But I do not want you to be ignorant, brethren, concerning those who have fallen asleep, lest you sorrow as others who have no hope. (1 Thessalonians 4:13 NKJV)

> And God will wipe away every tear from their eyes; there shall be no more death, nor sorrow, nor crying. There shall be no more pain, for the former things have passed away. (Revelations 21:4 NKJV)

Grief or sorrow is something that is common to everyone. At one time or the other, every person has been confronted with losing someone or something they love. Some grieve over wayward children or the death of a pet. Regardless of the source of grief, the Bible passage above warns us not to "sorrow as others who have no hope." It is not God's will that you be weighed down with grief because there is no grief in Him. When you are in the presence of the Lord, you experience His joy, peace, love, and much more.

God understands the pain of sorrow because He too has experienced it. When Jesus was hung on the cross, Isaiah 53:3 (KJV) states that He was "despised and rejected of men; a man of sorrows, and acquainted with grief." The grieving process is handled differently from person to person. Some people grieve for a few months while others mourn for the rest of their lives. Grief begins with a lowness of spirit and will eventually escalate to deep depression if it is not properly dealt with. Many people today are suffering from a major depressive disorder because of prolonged grief.

How do you deal with grief, then? How do you reverse the destructive cycle it can create? By having your hope in God. God has promised in Revelations 21:4 (NJKV) that there is a day in the near future when He will recreate heaven and earth, and His glorious presence will so fill the atmosphere that there will no longer be a cause to sorrow, cry, or weep. He also promises that there will be no more death. While we wait for that day to approach, God wants to pull you out of the grief you're in right now. Whether or not the person you've lost is a Christian, have hope in God that He has a better life for you than the one you're currently living. He has a great purpose and plan for your life and wants you to begin living it out today. Stop dwelling in the grief of the past. You cannot change what has happened, but you can change how it's affecting your life. Allow today to be a fresh start for you. Have hope in the God who believes in you. Please repeat this prayer out loud:

> Dear heavenly Father, I come to You in Jesus's name and give You this grief I've been tormented with. I renounce every attachment to it, and I declare that from

this day forward, I will no longer dwell on what has happened. I place my hope and trust in You today, and I thank You for the bright future You have in store for me. I receive my healing from grief and desire to have joy again. I thank You for leading me into Your perfect will for my life from this day on, in Jesus's name. Amen.

Scripture reading: Isaiah 53:1–6; 1 Thessalonians 4:13–18; Revelation 21:1–5

DAY 21   THE LIFE OF JESUS IN YOU WILL OVERCOME INTENSE PRESSURE

We are hard-pressed on every side, yet not crushed; we are perplexed, but not in despair; persecuted, but not forsaken; struck down, but not destroyed; always carrying about in the body the dying of the Lord Jesus, that the life of Jesus also may be manifested in our body. For we who live are always delivered to death for Jesus' sake, that the life of Jesus also may be manifested in our mortal flesh. (2 Corinthians 4:8–11 NKJV)

Have you ever been in a situation where there was literally no way of escape? Trouble that you thought would only last for a short period of time dragged on for months or even years. You felt boxed in on every side, one calamity or distressing situation after another, and you felt that you had no strength left in you. The pressure around you was so intense that it took effort to even breathe. Like many of us, the apostle Paul experienced this type of pressure. He was greatly persecuted for preaching about Jesus Christ and constantly faced situations where his life was at risk; and he didn't know exactly how God would come through for him. At times, he was severely beaten, thrown in jail, fastened in stocks, ridiculed by his peers, and heavily criticized. But you know what kept him going? His profound understanding of the life of Jesus in him.

The life of Jesus in him was "the light of the knowledge of the glory of God" (2 Corinthians 4:6 NKJV). In other words, the presence of Jesus in his life revealed and demonstrated the manifested presence and power of God and what that power could do to deliver him. He had such confidence that God would continually strengthen him, no matter what he faced, and it gave him tremendous hope to keep moving forward.

You should be encouraged today to know that if you have Jesus living in your heart, the presence of the most high God goes with you, no matter what you're facing. The power of God will strengthen, refresh, uplift, and propel you to go further and not give up on life. It will greatly encourage you to keep trusting in God until you experience full victory over the enormous adversity you're facing—whether it's related to your physical health, your emotional stability, family issues, job difficulties, and more. Jesus came that you may have life and have it more abundantly (John 10:10 NKJV). The life of Jesus in you will always deliver you out of the intense pressures of life. Please pray the following prayer out loud:

Dear heavenly Father, I come to You in the name of Jesus to thank You for the life of Jesus, which was deposited in my heart when I made Jesus Christ my Lord and Savior. I receive that life now and thank You that it flows throughout my body, from the top of my head to the soles of my feet. It also is moving on the intense circumstances that I am facing, to deliver me out of all of them. I thank You for all this now, in Jesus's name. Amen.

Scripture reading: John 10:1–11; 2 Corinthians 4:1–18

DAY 22   FORGET YOUR PAST

> Brethren, I do not count myself to have apprehended; but one thing I do, forgetting those things which are behind and reaching forward to those things which are ahead, I press toward the goal for the prize of the upward call of God in Christ Jesus. (Philippians 3:13–14 NKJV)

Have you ever had an afternoon when you sat down in your usual chair and reminisced about the past? You remembered all of the trips you took, the people you met, or even the things you said that you shouldn't have said. You may have regretted some of the decisions you made, especially if they involved another person. Many people today are still dealing with painful regret over their past mistakes, unresolved issues, or unfulfilled dreams. God wants you to stop dwelling on them and, instead, to focus on Him so that you may fulfill the purpose and plan He has for your life. Even if you did not have past regrets, living in past victories and never moving forward will stunt your growth as an individual. The apostle Paul had a lot of accomplishments he could have bragged about: his family pedigree, his higher learning, and his zeal. But he found something better than that. He made it his aim to forget about the past and reach forward to the things of God in order of fulfill his destiny.

Begin today. Don't ponder over all that happened to you in your past. Don't live any longer in the good old days either. Life can be better for you. Those skills and talents you've let wane, pick them back up again. Those dreams and desires you've let go of, rekindle them. Allow God to use you right now, where you are. Don't draw back. Don't allow thoughts of fear to keep you from moving forward unto the plan God has for you. Don't be filled with discouragement over what hasn't worked; instead, fill your imagination with what you desire God to do for you and then work toward fulfilling it. Even if you're in a sick bed right now, start dreaming of the life you want, not the life you've had. It is never too late for you to start over. God is a God of new beginnings. Even if you're ninety years old, like Sarah in the Bible, God can restore your years, strengthen your physical body, and give you the ability to fulfill His purpose for your life. Stop regretting the past or remaining satisfied with past victories. Keep moving forward. Please pray the following prayer out loud:

> Dear heavenly Father, I come to You in Jesus's name to present to You the painful regret of my past: my failures, fears, unfulfilled dreams, people I've hurt, poor decisions I've made, or (fill in the blank). I forgive myself for the part I played and thank You for forgiving me for not fulfilling my destiny. I now give my life to You to use me for Your glory and receive my healing and full restoration now in Jesus's name. Amen.

Scripture reading: Isaiah 43:18–19; Romans 4:16–25; Philippians 3:1–14; Revelations 21:1–5

DAY 23 HEALING FROM TUMORS AND INCURABLE DISEASES

The Lord will afflict you with the boils of Egypt and with tumors, scurvy, and the itch, from which you cannot be cured. (Deuteronomy 28:27 NLT)

But Christ has rescued us from the curse pronounced by the law. When He was hung on the cross, He took upon Himself the curse of our wrongdoing. For it is written in the Scriptures, "Cursed is everyone who is hung on a tree." Through Christ Jesus, God has blessed the Gentiles with the same blessing He promised to Abraham, so that we who are believers might receive the promised Holy Spirit through faith. (Galatians 3:13–14 NLT)

Many people today are suffering from incurable diseases such as HIV, autoimmune disorders, and malignant tumors or cancer and have lost hope of ever getting better. For some people, their physicians have pronounced a death sentence and told them that they only have a few months left to live. A looming cloud hangs over their heads daily, and they are gripped with fear for themselves and what will happen to their loved ones after they're gone. Others believe their doctor's report to the point that they've even begun to make arrangements for their own funerals. If this describes you in any way, don't give up just yet. The Bible passage above says that Jesus Christ "rescued us from the curse pronounced by the law … and has blessed the Gentiles with the same blessing He promised to Abraham" (Galatians 3:13–14 NLT). The curse was the penalty of breaking the Old Testament Law. In a nutshell, it encompassed all poverty, barrenness, sickness, incurable diseases, and more.

You may read Deuteronomy 28 and ask, "How can a loving God be associated with blessing and cursing?" Well, He's not. God is the source of every earthly and heavenly blessing, and His will is to bless you beyond your wildest dreams. He desires to give you a life more amazing than you ever expected, to give you great health, and to prosper you, your family, your bank accounts, your job, and every work of your hands. The curse came on the earth the day that Adam sinned against God; Satan is the source of that curse. God gives each of us the choice to choose "between life and death, between blessings and curses" (Deuteronomy 30:19 NLT). When you choose to obey the Lord and accept Jesus as your Lord and Savior, you are no longer under the influence of the curse and the author of that curse, Satan. Instead, you now have access to the everlasting life of God, and that life will flow through you to get rid of every abnormality in your body, including tumors and other incurable diseases. It will purge out every self-destructive cell in your body until you are perfectly whole.

Don't make your doctor's report the final word. Make Jesus's report the final word. His report says that you are redeemed from all poverty, all sickness, and all incurable diseases. Start creating mental images of you being whole. Begin to see yourself in perfect health. When you place your confidence in God, He will never fail you. Please pray the following prayer out loud:

> Dear heavenly Father, I come to You in Jesus's name to acknowledge that Jesus is my Lord and Savior. Therefore, I am redeemed from this incurable disease (fill in the blank). I receive the blessing of God operating in my life and thank You that it's Your perfect will to restore me back to perfect health. I receive my healing now and declare that I am healed from this incurable disease in Jesus's name. Amen.

Scripture reading: Genesis 3:1–16; Deuteronomy 28:1–27; Deuteronomy 30:1–20; Galatians 3:1–14

DAY 24   WHY CURSING IS DETRIMENTAL TO YOUR HEALTH

As he loved cursing, so let it come to him; as he did not delight in blessing, so let it be far from him. (Psalm 109:17 NKJV)

I call heaven and earth as witnesses today against you, that I have set before you life and death, blessing and cursing; therefore choose life, that both you and your descendants may live." (Deuteronomy 30:19 NKJV)

Remember when you were a child and, just to be a cool kid, you imitated what you heard your classmates say? They used profanity in every other word they spoke, and you wanted to be just like them. Or maybe that wasn't your experience. Perhaps you only use profanity when under stress and have tried to stop but find it difficult. You may also say, "I never use profanity when I speak!" This may be true, but do you say terrible things about people behind their back or to their faces? Do you have trouble controlling your tongue when people address you the wrong way and lash out bitterly at them? You may not know it, but you've just cursed them. To curse people is more than just using profanity; it is directing words at them that promote and empower failure in their lives. What's worse is that as you curse people, you curse yourself at the same time (Psalm 109:17 NKJV).

To bless people, on the other hand, is to speak words over them that will promote and empower their success in life. When God blessed Adam, He spoke the following words, which enabled Adam to succeed in the assignment that He had for him: "Be fruitful, and multiply, and replenish the earth" (Genesis 1:28 KJV). God relegates the choice of your words to you, but encourages you to "choose life, that both you and your descendants may live" (Deuteronomy 30:19 NKJV). Cursing people and even yourself attracts the curse and, consequently, death, while blessing yourself and other people attracts the blessing and, consequently, life. Many people are sick today because they have spent years tearing others apart with their words. Others have declared words over themselves like, "I'll never live past sixty years," or, "It goes downhill when you reach your sixties," or, "I don't want to get old." It's no wonder that such people have declining health as they reach their sixties and seventies. God desires you to live a long and fulfilled life. Start paying attention to the words that you speak over yourself and other people. Speak kindly to yourself and others. You were created to bless and not curse.

Please pray the following prayer out loud:

Dear heavenly Father, I come to You in Jesus's name to repent from the negative words I have spoken over myself and others. I forgive myself for what I have said over my own body and will do my best to make amends with the people I have hurt with my words. I receive my forgiveness now and thank You for my healing in Jesus's name. Amen.

Scripture reading: Psalm 109:17; James 3:1–12; 1 Peter 3:8–12

DAY 25 UNUSUAL MIRACLES FOR BLIND EYES

He answered and said, "A Man called Jesus made clay and anointed my eyes and said to me, 'Go to the pool of Siloam and wash.' So I went and washed, and I received my sight." (John 9:11 NKJV)

Most people seldom believe in miracles today, especially when it pertains to something that seems impossible. They may profess that they believe in miracles when small things are concerned, things that involve little risk. Some can believe in a miracle in their job or family environment, but for something like blindness, forget it! What makes it even more challenging is when blindness occurs at birth and it's the only state that person has ever known. The man who Jesus performed a miracle for was blind from birth and had never even seen his own parents. As Jesus passed by him one day, He did something that was unusual and a little disgusting to us today. He spat on the ground full of sand and made a little clay out of the spit/sand mixture. He rubbed it over the man's eyes and instructed him to go wash it off at the pool of Siloam. Someone may have led him to the pool. After he obeyed Jesus's instructions, he was able to see clearly for the first time.

You may ask, "Why didn't Jesus just place His hands over the man's eyes to heal him?" Because this was how the Father instructed Him to do it. You may have been diagnosed with an eye disorder such as macular degeneration, cataract, glaucoma, or diabetic retinopathy, and you've noticed that your eyesight has greatly diminished. You may have exhausted all of the medical options you once had, such as prescription glasses, medications, or surgery, and now are left to face the hard fact that your eyes may never get better. I'm here to bring you good news. Jesus specializes in unusual miracles for blind eyes. His desire to perform a miracle on your behalf is not based on how good you are or how horrible a person you've been. It is based on His great love for you. What's even more amazing is that He's not limited to the stage of your disease; it's just as easy for Him to correct your eyes if all you need are reading glasses as it is for Him perform total surgery on your failed eyesight. In fact, one of His chief assignments while He was on the earth was to facilitate the "recovery of sight to the blind" through the power of the Holy Spirit (Luke 4:18 NKJV).

That same Holy Spirit is in you if you've made Jesus your Lord and Savior. That same anointing power of God to perform miracles, which was on Jesus, is in you. How did Jesus maintain a constant stream of the power of God flowing in His life? By continuously meditating on scripture. Proverbs 4:20 (NKJV) states, "My son, give attention to my words; incline your ears to my sayings. Do not let them depart from your eyes; keep them in the midst of your heart; for they are life to those who find them, and health to all their flesh." Even if you can't see the words of scripture to read them, have someone read them to you constantly. Meditate on healing scriptures as often as you can throughout the day. Jesus is still the same healer today as He was back then. You access His healing for your eyes by constantly meditating on the Word of God, particularly on healing scriptures, all of which this thirty-day devotional consists of.

Please pray the following prayer out loud:

> Dear heavenly Father, I come to You in the name of Jesus to receive the full recovery of my eyesight. I believe that it's Your perfect will for me to be whole, and I claim my miracle now. Thank You for restoring my eyesight, and I walk in my miracle and healing now in Jesus's name. Amen.

Scripture reading: Psalm 13:1–6; Psalm 119:17–18; Isaiah 42:1–7; Luke 4:17–18

DAY 26   GOD'S DIVINE REMEDY FOR THE HEARING-IMPAIRED

"Say to those who are fearful-hearted, be strong, do not fear! Behold your God will come with vengeance, with the recompense of God; He will come and save you." Then the eyes of the blind shall be opened, and the ears of the deaf shall be unstopped. (Isaiah 35:4–5 NKJV)

He awakens Me morning by morning, He awakens My ear to hear as the learned. The Lord God has opened my ear. (Isaiah 50:4 NKJV)

Hearing is so natural to most of us that we often don't even consider it until a problem occurs. The ability to hear is not properly valued because it occurs without effort for many of us. Young people, especially, enjoy loud, blasting music and do not heed their parents advice to lower the volume of their music players. Hearing impairments are increasing and are especially prevalent today among the elderly. In fact, there is a common saying that when one gets old, "hearing goes." Hearing aids are often used to help amplify sound so that a greater level of hearing can be achieved, but they are not a permanent cure. Unlike the modern remedy of hearing aids, God's remedy is quite transformational. He can perform a creative miracle to open deaf ears. In the first passage above, He promises to unstop or unplug the ears of the deaf. According to Merriam-Webster's dictionary, to unstop is "to make passage through (something) possible by removing obstructions." It also means "to clear, free, and open."

You may not fully comprehend the inner workings of your ear, how sound is created, or the true cause of your hearing impairment, but that doesn't matter. What matters is that God can and will open your ears so that you may hear again. This applies to you if you are slightly hearing-impaired or completely deaf. Furthermore, God can enable your ears to hear perfectly "as the learned." Don't be concerned any longer about your hearing. You have access to Someone who knows how your ears work, how they ought to work, and how to get them working again. Just ask Him. Please pray the following prayer out loud:

Dear heavenly Father, I come to You in the name of Jesus to present to You this hearing impairment. I desire to be fully restored of my hearing and believe, with all my heart, that You are my healer. I receive my healing now, and I thank You for it in Jesus's name. Amen.

Scripture reading: Isaiah 35:1–6; Isaiah 50:1–5; Matthew 13:1–16

DAY 27   VICTORY OVER SPEECH DISORDERS

Then the lame shall leap like a deer, and the tongue of the dumb sing. (Isaiah 35:6 NKJV)

The Lord God has given Me the tongue of the learned, that I should know how to speak a word in season to him who is weary. (Isaiah 50:4 NKJV)

We have all experienced moments of being tongue-tied, where we temporarily couldn't communicate effectively, either because of shyness, stage fright, or shock over a situation. For many people today, however, speech disorders, such as difficulty articulating words, stuttering, slurred speech, or muteness, are a consistent problem. Several people experience difficulty with their speech because of a hearing impairment from childhood. Speech disorders affect them socially, as they often shy away from people or public oration. No matter what is wrong with your tongue, God is able to give you the "tongue of the learned" and help you to speak clearly, enunciate your words properly, and deliver a complete thought. How am I so sure? I am so sure because He did it for me.

Growing up, I never had a clinically diagnosed speech problem, but I had a hard time speaking in public. I would get so nervous when I stood in front of people that my words would often come out jumbled. Often, my words were not coherent, and it was by the mercy of God that I made it through some of my earlier years of schooling. God taught me to speak a little more slowly so that I could enunciate my words. Like Isaiah 50:4 (NKJV), He opened my tongue and taught me how to speak to people more effectively.

If you're having difficulty with your speech, God desires to give you a new tongue—a tongue that not only articulates words but also speaks with wisdom. He wants to give you the ability to always say the right thing, especially when you're addressing other people. He created your tongue not just to speak words, but to speak effective words that bring comfort to others. He gave you a tongue so that you may worship Him, sing His praises, and give Him glory with it. I will pray the following prayer over you, and I ask you to agree:

Heavenly Father, in the name of Jesus, I come to You on the behalf of every person reading this devotional who has any type of difficulty with their speaking ability. I ask that their tongues be loosed and that You would give them divine utterance so that they may speak more eloquently, clearly, and effectively. I ask that You would fill their tongue with the tongue of the learned and give them wisdom on their word choices. I thank You that it gives You great pleasure to give us good gifts (Matthew 7:11 NKJV). I thank You for their healing now, in Jesus's name. Amen.

Scripture reading: Isaiah 35:6; Isaiah 51:15–16; Jeremiah 1:1–10; Luke 12:11–12

DAY 28 — SHAVE OFF THE SHAME OF YOUR PAST

> Then Pharaoh sent and called Joseph, and they brought him hastily out of the dungeon. But Joseph [first] shaved himself, changed his clothes, and made himself presentable; then he came to Pharaoh's presence. (Genesis 41:14 Amplified Bible, Classic Edition)

Many of you have been diligently reading each day's topic and gleaning from the different areas of healing that have been addressed. You may even be excited about what you've heard so far, particularly that God loves you and desires for you to be whole, spirit, soul, and body. Others reading this material may be surprised at how quickly their healing has manifested and how much better they feel compared to the beginning of this book. I caution you, however, to give attention to what I'm about to say. Until you get rid of your past, you can't step into the glorious future God has in store for you. In the passage above, Joseph had been thrown into jail because of a false accusation made by Pharaoh's wife. She wanted to commit adultery with Joseph, and when he refused her repeated advances, she accused him of attempted rape. He remained in jail for a crime that he did not commit, and even though his future looked bleak, God was developing his leadership skills there.

At the appointed time, Pharaoh experienced a problem that he had no natural answer for. He had two dreams he didn't understand the meaning of and sought someone who could interpret them. Before entering the king's presence, he "[first] shaved himself, changed his clothes, and made himself presentable" (Genesis 41:14 AMPC). Joseph shaved off the evidence of shame from being in jail for the past two years. He took off the garments of humiliation (the prison garments) and put on clothing that now reflected what he was about to become. When he stood in the presence of the king, he was no longer in rags but was appropriately clothed. As he stood there before the king, he was immediately elevated from a former position of lowliness to a position of high esteem, honor, and restoration.

Right now, the King of Kings, Jesus Christ, has begun the process of healing in you. He has elevated you from a position of shame, humiliation, low self-esteem, sickness, and poverty to a position of restored dignity, restored health, and restored wealth. Don't drag the pain of your past with you. Don't believe the lie of the devil that nothing has changed in you. Whether you've experienced it or not, God's healing has already begun to take place in you, and you will experience complete victory over what you are facing or have faced. As Joseph made the decision to shave himself, so you too must make the decision to not look back at all the past failed attempts to receive your healing. Stop thinking that your situation is hopeless; with God, you will always have hope. Also, do not allow the people around you to keep reminding you of your past. Instead, remind them that Jesus Christ paid for your healing while He was on the cross, that you've already received your healing, and that you are walking out the process of that healing.

Please pray the following prayer out loud:

> Dear heavenly Father, I come to You in the name of Jesus to stand on the healing that Jesus has purchased for me on the cross. I shave off all the fear, doubt, depression, unbelief, and negative thinking. I remove every garment of shame and sickness with which I was once clothed, and I now put on healing garments, praise garments, restoration garments, and dignity garments. I thank You for my gift now, in Jesus's name. Amen.

Scriptural reading: Genesis 41:1–57; Isaiah 61:1–11; Ephesians 4:20–24

DAY 29 STAND FAST IN YOUR HEALING

> Stand fast therefore in the liberty by which Christ has made us free, and do not
> be entangled again with a yoke of bondage. (Galatians 5:1 NKJV)

Freedom comes with a great price. We all know that many of the freedoms that we enjoy here in America came because of the men and women who fought for them. We enjoy the freedom of speech, freedom of religion, and the freedom to pursue our dreams. We are free to walk down the street, free to laugh, free to take family vacations, and more. Freedom, as great as it is when it's present, doesn't happen automatically; it has to be fought for and properly maintained. Jesus Christ fought for our spiritual freedom when He was on the cross and obtained it when He was resurrected. He purchased your salvation, healing, prosperity, and everything that pertains to you having an abundant life here on the earth. The Holy Spirit, speaking through Paul, warns us to "stand fast therefore in the liberty by which Christ has made us free" and not to become "entangled again with a yoke of bondage" (Galatians 5:1 NKJV).

If you have made Jesus Christ your Lord and Savior, you are now responsible for holding fast to every gift He's made available to you. Particularly where your healing is concern, you have to stand your ground and refuse to allow the enemy to gain a foothold into your life, causing you to stumble. Every healing that has already taken place in your mind and body is designed to be permanent, but that healing can sometimes wane if you are ignorant to some of Satan's tactics to attempt to bring you back into a state of bondage (sickness, disease, etc). Some of his famous tactics are reminding you of past struggles, accusing you of things that God has already forgiven you for, offense, doubt, and fear. Offense can literally bring you back to the state you once were in before you received your healing. It can lower your body's defense mechanisms, therefore putting you at risk of being ill again. Fear is the enemy's greatest tactic to steal your joy and rob you of your healing. Since fear is specific to each person, you will have to stand your ground in Christ in order to overcome it. What makes one person afraid may not necessarily frighten another person, so know yourself.

Develop yourself in the love of God and don't be so quick to be offended. Refuse to believe the worst of people, even when you know how terribly they behave. Instead, choose to believe the best of every person. Love one another, and be quick to forgive. Refuse to believe the lies of Satan as he tries to fill your mind with fear. Stand fast in the freedom that is already yours. Please pray the following prayer out loud:

> Heavenly Father, I come boldly to Your throne to obtain the grace to stand fast
> in my healing. I am not ignorant of Satan's devices to try to steal my healing
> by reminding me of my past mistakes, causing me to be offended at others and

bringing doubtful and fearful thoughts to my mind. I refused to yield to the enemy's tactics to steal my healing. I thank You for the grace to love others and forgive quickly so that I may be able to keep my healing. I pray all of this now in Jesus's name.

Scripture reading: Galatians 1–26; 2 Corinthians 2:1–11; Ephesians 4:17–27

DAY 30   PRACTICAL STEPS TO MAINTAINING YOUR HEALING

> This Book of the Law shall not depart from your mouth, but you shall meditate in it day and night, that you may observe to do according to all that is written in it. For then you will make your way prosperous, and then you will have good success. (Joshua 1:8 NKJV)

God has always been very practical in the ways in which He's dealt with mankind. In the beginning, He placed Adam and Eve in a beautiful garden called Eden and gave them simple instructions that they could eat of all the fruit trees except for the tree of the knowledge of good and evil. As easy as that instruction was, they disobeyed. Later on Deuteronomy 28:1–2 (AMPC), He told the children of Israel the following: "If you will listen diligently to the voice of the Lord you God, being watchful to do all His commandments which I command you this day, the Lord your God will set you high above all the nations of the earth. And all these blessings shall come upon you and overtake you if you heed the voice of the Lord your God."

When you read the Bible, have a listening ear. Don't assume you've heard it before, and take every word as if it were God speaking to you directly because that is the reality. God's first instruction to Joshua and the children of Israel was not to allow the book of the Law to leave their mouths. When you read the healing scriptures provided, say them out loud so that your ears can make a connection with what you're reading. Take each verse line by line and ponder how it can be applied to your situation. The next part of the instruction was to "meditate in it day and night" (Joshua 1:8 NKJV). Establish the habit of spending time in God's Word when you first get up in the morning. Even if it's for only fifteen minutes, set aside that time. Get up earlier in the morning if you have to. Also, before you go to bed, read those scriptures over yourself again and again. If you are up for a challenge, spend time with the Lord three times a day. Just as you eat three meals a day, ingest three meals of the Word of God daily.

Observing the Word of God is another key aspect to maintaining your healing. It's more than just reading healing scriptures; it is paying close, watchful attention to what is being said. In other words, it involves constantly keeping the Word of God before your eyes to look at it. Proverbs 4:21–22 (AMPC) instructs you to "let them not depart from your sight; keep them in the center of your heart. For they are life to those who find them, healing and health to all their flesh." This is God's formula for success in your healing and having a prosperous life: speaking the Word of God, meditating on it all through the day, and keeping it constantly before your eyes that you may do what it says. I challenge you to go over this thirty-day devotional again and apply these principles. You will be amazed at the results you get.

Scripture reading: Joshua 1:1–9; Proverbs 4:20–23; John 14:21–24; John 15:1–8

Printed in the United States
By Bookmasters